Walt Disney

Snow White
and the Seven Dwarfs

Adapted by Rita Balducci
Illustrated by Don Williams

A GOLDEN BOOK • NEW YORK
Western Publishing Company, Inc., Racine, Wisconsin 53404

Once there was a fair young princess named Snow White. She lived in a palace in a faraway kingdom with her cruel stepmother, the Queen.

As time passed, the Queen became jealous of Snow White's beauty. She made the young girl dress in rags and work in the kitchen. In spite of her hard life, Snow White remained good and kind and cheerful.

The wicked Queen had a magic mirror that
would answer any question. Every day she stood
before the mirror and asked,

"Magic mirror on the wall,
Who is the fairest one of all?"

And the mirror always answered that the Queen
was the fairest in the kingdom.

But the day came at last when the mirror
answered,

> "Her lips rose red, her hair like night,
> Her skin like snow, her name—
> Snow White!"

The Queen was furious. "I will destroy the
girl!" she shrieked.

The Queen called one of her huntsmen to her. "Take Snow White deep into the forest and kill her," she ordered.

The unhappy huntsman took Snow White deep into the forest, but he could not kill the lovely princess. He told Snow White of the Queen's wicked plan.

"You must run and hide!" the good man begged her. "You can never come back."

Poor Snow White! She ran through the woods, tripping over branches and roots. The forest was dark and frightening. Strange shadows moved around her, and glowing eyes watched her. She ran and ran.

At last some friendly animals found Snow
White and led her to a cottage in a clearing.
"Maybe I can stay here," she said hopefully.
Snow White knocked on the door.

There was no one at home. Slowly Snow White
opened the door.

"Oh, my goodness!" she said when she looked
around the tiny room. There were dirty dishes on
the table, and dust was everywhere.

"I will tidy up," Snow White said as she started sweeping the floor. "Maybe the people who live here will let me keep house for them."

Snow White worked all afternoon. Then she was so tired that she went upstairs and lay down across several of the little beds she found. Soon she was fast asleep.

Not far away, the seven dwarfs who lived in the cottage had just finished their day's work. They left the jewel mine where they worked and marched home together in a line—Doc, Happy, Grumpy, Sleepy, Sneezy, Bashful, and at the very end of the line, Dopey.

As they walked, they sang,

"Heigh-ho, heigh-ho,
It's home from work we go . . ."

When the dwarfs entered the cottage, they were amazed to see how neat and clean it was.

"Someone's been in our house!" said Grumpy. "Maybe it's a ghost or a goblin, and maybe it's still here!"

Upstairs the dwarfs found Snow White fast
asleep. Suddenly Sneezy sneezed. Snow White
woke with a start. She was amazed to see the seven
little men.

Snow White explained to the dwarfs that she
was in terrible danger. The dwarfs told her that
she would be safe if she stayed with them.

Meanwhile the Queen had learned from her
magic mirror that Snow White was still alive—
and living with the seven dwarfs. The Queen used
her evil powers to change herself into an old
woman. Then she filled a basket with apples,
placing a poisoned one on top.

The next morning the evil Queen waited until the dwarfs had left the cottage. Then she spoke to Snow White. "Have an apple, dearie," she said. "Taste it."

The innocent young princess took one bite and fell to the ground.

The dwarfs learned what had happened from the birds and animals. They ran back to the cottage as fast as they could and saw the old woman running away. They chased the wicked Queen to the top of a rocky cliff.

Suddenly the sky grew dark. Thunder boomed and lightning flashed, splitting the cliff in two. The evil Queen slipped and fell to her doom. She was gone forever.

Snow White was in a deep and endless sleep.
The dwarfs were very sad. They built a coffin of
glass and gold for the beautiful princess and kept
watch over her day and night.

One day a handsome prince came riding by. He had heard stories about the lovely princess asleep in the forest. When he saw Snow White, he fell in love with her. He leaned over her and kissed her.

Suddenly Snow White opened her eyes. She smiled at the prince beside her. Love's first kiss had broken the evil spell.

The seven dwarfs danced with joy. Snow White was alive! Soon the dwarfs were waving good-bye. Snow White rode off with the prince to his castle, where they lived happily ever after.